JACQUES-HENRI LARTIGUE

BOY WITH A CAMERA BY JOHN CECH

FOUR WINDS PRESS ❋ NEW YORK

MAXWELL MACMILLAN CANADA   TORONTO   MAXWELL MACMILLAN INTERNATIONAL   NEW YORK   OXFORD   SINGAPORE   SYDNEY

For Jack Nichelson,
    who shared his Lartigue enthusiasm
    and struck the spark for this project, and
for Carol Murphy,
    who so generously
    helped me translate it into a reality

—J.C.

ACKNOWLEDGMENTS

I wish to send a very special note of thanks to Martine d'Astier, artistic and administrative director of L'Association des Amis de Jacques-Henri Lartigue, for her most generous and enthusiastic support of this project, and to her assistant, Ann Marie Cousin, for her ever-timely, ever-gracious help in the preparation of this book.

    I am deeply grateful to L'Association des Amis de Jacques-Henri Lartigue and to La Mission du Patrimoine photographique du Ministère de la Culture of the Republic of France for their permission to reprint the Lartigue photographs and journal excerpts that appear in this volume.

First edition   Printed and bound in the United States of America.   1 0   9   8   7   6   5   4   3   2   1   The text of this book is set in Gill Light. Book design by Christy Hale Library of Congress Cataloging-in-Publication Data   Cech, John.   Jacques-Henri Lartigue : boy with a camera / by John Cech.   p.   cm.   1. Lartigue, Jacques-Henri, 1894–   Juvenile literature. 2. Photographers—France—Biography—Juvenile literature.   [1.Lartigue, Jacques-Henri, 1894–   2. Photographers.]   1. Title.   TR140.L32C43   1994   770'.92—dc20   [B]   94-10210 ISBN 0-02-718136-7

For his seventh birthday, in 1902, Jacques-Henri Lartigue's father gave him the only present that he truly wanted: a camera of his own.

It was a beautiful Gaumont, made of wood and brass, and it sat upon a tripod. Jacques had to stand on a stool to use it. The first picture that he took completely by himself was this one of his family in front of their house. In the back row, from the left, there's his Aunt Yé-Yé, his Uncle August, and Papa and Mama Lartigue, and in the front, little André on his bike, Jacques's brother Maurice (whom everyone called Zissou), and cousin Marcelle happily holding Jacques's kitten, Zizi.

Jacques learned from his father how to load the camera with the glass plates on which the pictures would later be developed. He knew how to duck his head under the black cloth at the back of the camera to focus the upside-down image that appeared there, and then, while everyone stood perfectly still, he took the cork off the lens and counted the seconds: one, two, three . . . et voilà!

Here are his cousins Bouboutte, Louis, and Robert, and his brother Zissou modeling their Mardi Gras masks.

"Photography is something you learn to love very quickly," Jacques wrote in the diary he began keeping almost as soon as he could write. "I know that many, many things are going to ask me to have their pictures taken and I will take them all."

And he did. He took hundreds and hundreds of pictures.

He used his camera to record what he saw, but he didn't stop there. He played with his camera, looking for new, unusual ways to take pictures with it. For this photograph of his toy cars, he placed his camera right on the rug so that the cars seem to race across the floor.

Jacques called photography
"a magic thing." Photographs were
little miracles. A photograph could
capture an instant in time, even
stop something in motion. This
magic could hold a ball forever
suspended in the air above the
head of his nanny, Dudu,

it could see the blur his brother
Zissou became when he bounced
the same ball off his head,

and it could perform tricks. In this photographic experiment, Zissou is dressed as a ghost on the porch steps *and* he is waving from the bench in the same frame of film—a double exposure.

Dudu clicked the shutter for this self-portrait of Jacques pretending to be asleep, with Zizi the kitten tucked under the covers with him.

Soon Jacques had a smaller camera that took pictures in less time. Still, it was heavy, and his mother worried that he might hurt himself, since he carried the camera with him everywhere on a strap over his shoulder. But Jacques did not mind the weight; it meant a camera full of pictures.

In April of 1904, he hiked across the sand dunes near the channel between France and England, where his family was on vacation. He never forgot how his heart was pounding when he took this picture (the only one!) of a great success: the first public flight of an airplane in France . . . Gabriel Voisin soaring twenty yards in his glider. Then, later that same day, Jacques also recorded his Uncle Raymond showing how this mighty deed had been done.

Every moment of life was an adventure for Jacques, and he used his camera to save these scenes as they flashed by. He made photographs at the beach, where he filled his pictures with cousins, friends, sailboats, straw hats, and a very wet spaniel; in the parks of Paris, where he watched a pony practicing how to count; and on the city's boulevards, where he photographed the ladies promenading in all their feathery finery.

Jacques observed the world through eyes that loved invention and daring and speed.

Fabulous automobiles were beginning to rush along the roads. And racing cars like this Delage, which Jacques saw with his father, could travel at the fantastic speed of thirty-five miles per hour! Jacques followed the automobile down the course and snapped this picture that made the tires stretch with speed.

The Lartigues and their large family and many friends were all swept up in the sheer excitement of trying out the latest inventions and discoveries. No one, no matter how old, seemed to have forgotten how to play. The huge kites that they flew sometimes took two or three people to control.

Zissou took an old bicycle and some boards and built a paddleboat that was sailed by everyone in the pool at their country home. Because Jacques was too young, his mother did not allow him to take part in some of these risky ventures. So he watched and photographed.

But Jacques's mother was not watching one day when he climbed aboard one of the "bobs" that Zissou created from some bicycle tires, some pipes, and a steering wheel. Jacques joined in the races and went careening down the hill. Who knows how he managed to take this picture and hold on, too. Later, he also caught the gravel-churning turns, the bent wheels on Zissou's "bob," and the long, slow climb back up the hill.

Ever since Zissou had seen Gabriel Voisin sail over the dunes, he had wanted to fly. And so, after his early experiments with an umbrella, he built glider after glider, often using the family bedsheets to stretch across the framework of the wings. Jacques, of course, recorded all of these events with his camera, from the first jumps, to the many repairs and refinements, to the remarkable flight of Zissou in his ZYX 24.

Not all of Zissou's inventions required heroic feats. Here, he is trying out the latest in inner tubes. This one had rubber legs and feet built into it so that he could wear his suit and tie while floating in the water.

Because there was always a chance that a picture might not turn out in development, Jacques would draw small sketches of the scenes he'd photographed (like the one of Zissou) at the bottoms of the pages of his diaries. Above the drawings, he reported on the weather, what he dreamed the night before, and exactly what he did each day.

Wherever Jacques turned his camera, he found
moments of play, moments of happiness, moments
of wonder to save on film: his family and friends
      playing tennis
      vaulting
      twirling
      diving
      backflipping and

flying.

And the sight of all these sent his spirit soaring.

A BIOGRAPHICAL NOTE ABOUT JACQUES-HENRI LARTIGUE

Jacques-Henri Lartigue was born in Paris on June 13, 1894. He was the second son in a prosperous family. His father, Henri Lartigue, had founded a major newspaper in France and had helped to finance a railroad that was built across North Africa. The elder Lartigue was himself a very accomplished amateur photographer as well as a fan of, and participant in, such sports of the day as aviating, automobile racing, hot-air ballooning, giant kite flying, and tennis. He eagerly passed on to his sons these enthusiasms for the new, the novel, and the inventive that were occurring all around them in what has been called the belle epoque—the "beautiful time"—in France during the first two decades of the twentieth century. Lartigue's pictures are regarded as the most vivid document of that supremely creative time before the tragedy of World War I changed the face and mood of Europe.

While Lartigue was still quite young, his mother became concerned about how much money he was spending on the photographic plates, which he ran to the local pharmacy daily to buy. He promised her that he would stop taking pictures when he was eighteen years old. Thank goodness that he did not.

In fact, Lartigue went on in his long life to take more than a quarter of a million pictures, which he has since left as his legacy to the French nation. Though he took an extraordinary number of pictures of his family and friends, Lartigue thought of himself as simply an amateur photographer. His formal artistic training was as a painter, and this is how he wished to be known. It was not until late in his life, when he was nearly seventy years old, that his photographs were finally "discovered" and exhibited in 1963 by John Szarkowski, the director of the photography department of the Museum of Modern Art in New York. Szarkowski had seen the pictures Lartigue had taken and immediately recognized them as "the observations of a genius: fresh perceptions, poetically sensed and graphically fixed."

Since then, there have been many exhibitions of Lartigue's pictures, and his work is hailed as a national treasure in France. Indeed, his photographs are a remarkable gift to the rest of the world as well. The exuberant creative spirit he celebrates in his pictures transcends the limits of time and place to inspire us today—reminding us with laughter and awe to be sure to always let a part of ourselves remain playful and young.

Just a few years before his death in 1986 at the age of 92, Lartigue was asked by an interviewer if he regretted anything about his life. He responded, "Yes, that I don't have more talent. That I am not an angel." But having seen his photographs, we know that he was blessed with heavenly gifts!

LIST OF PHOTOGRAPHS